A SHORT HISTORY OF WARSASH

"F.W.L."

My grandfather, Frederick William Light, was born in Netley Abbey in 1864. When he was five years old, his father died, and his mother, Ann, moved with her family to Warsash. She bought a cottage in Fleet End Road name Tea Tree Cottage and started a laundry business. The old laundry is still in existence at the back of the cottage, now named Bay Tree Cottage.

Grandfather married Ellen Gray, a farmer's daughter from Hill Head, and bought two acres of land at the back of his mother's house, in Green Lane. There he built two cottages, and he and my grandmother cultivated the land, growing strawberries and other soft fruit. Grandmother kept chickens and sold the eggs at Fareham market. They had two daughters. Dora, the elder, and May, who was my mother.

Grandfather, for the greater part of his life, was an active member of Warsash Congregational Church. He also taught in the Sunday School. He was a founder member of Warsash Horticultural Society and an enthusiastic grower of sweet peas and prize vegetables.

In about 1937, concerned about changes in the village after Warsash House was demolished, and the estate sold for housing, grandfather began to put together a history of the village as he remembered it as a boy and young man; this book being the result. After it was published he began again to write, hoping to finish more memoirs for a book for my sister, Ruth.

He died in 1942 before it was completed, but the chapters he did write were kept by my mother and are included in this edition.

I would like to thank my cousin, Wyn Newbury, for the contribution of his collection of old photographs included in this book.

Jean Murton
1985

INTRODUCTORY

In attempting to write the history of a district with such widely spaced boundaries as Hook, Warsash, Newtown, and Fleetend, one has the choice of several methods. Perhaps the most usual is to describe its development in chronological order. This method, however, has the disadvantage that it is necessary to keep flitting from one part of the district to another so many times that it is apt to breed confusion in the mind of the reader, and he is left at the end with only a medley of broken pictures which leave no clear or lasting impression.

But the history of any district is always bound up very closely with its *roads*. I have therefore, in this necessarily fragmentary survey, thought it best first to give some general information about them and their development from as early a period as possible, afterward taking each main road in turn, and trying to portray the changes that have taken place on the road itself, on the various smaller roads leading from it, and of that particular portion of the district adjacent to them. We shall, I think, by this method, get a clearer and more comprehensive idea of the development of the district as a whole, and the many changes that have taken place in it during the period covered by this survey.

The information contained herein has been obtained from many and varied sources, and wherever possible has been verified by reference to those people whose knowledge of any particular portion of it may reasonably be regarded as authentic. Although there are many personal reminiscences, they all have some connection with and bearing upon the story of the period in which they occur; and may be explained by the fact that the history is written primarily for the benefit of my grand-daughter, Jean Murton, to whom it is dedicated. It will, I am sure, be read not without some pleasure and profit, by all those who take an intelligent interest in the place in which they live.

It will help us to understand better the story which we have to recount, if we remember that prior to the year 1864 (in which year I was born) a very large proportion of Warsash was common land. The common boundary was roughly as follows. From Warsash Corner to Havelock Road, down that road and along the back of Hamble Bank to the beginning of Ship's Bank on to Hook meadow and from that point almost in a straight line to Abshot Corner. From there to the Titchfield road and along that to Hook Gate and on through the Sluice and up to Pound Gate. From there it followed the course of the stream to Pest House and on the Park Gate turnpike. From here a wide stretch of common stretched right through to Sarisbury Green. The boundary ran along Cold East park, across Brook Lane to the West edge of Mr. Binstead's land. From this point it followed a small stream and footpath down to Narrow Bridge where it turned at right angles and ran almost in a straight line to Furze Cottage. At that point it turned right and ran by the road to Warsash Corner. It was known as Titchfield Common.

The numerous Commons Inclosure Acts which were passed by Parliament were designed to bring all common land in the country into cultivation so that where it had hitherto supported only a limited number of cattle for which it afforded rough grazing, it might in time produce food in quantities which would be more beneficial to the increasing population. When the Commons Inclosure Acts were applied to this particular district, between 1860 and 1864, the common land was controlled by the Vestry of Titchfield Church and this body engaged a number of men to share out the common amongst the ratepayers, who were the only ones entitled to receive a grant of land under the Acts. The land was to be apportioned according to the amount of rates paid, and the task was a very difficult one. The working out of the Acts inevitably resulted in many hardships and inequalities. The comparatively rich received still more land, the poor, none at all. In this district there were a number of people who did hire-carting, mostly haulage of timber. One man I know went to Portsmouth market with poultry, eggs, vegetables and fruit. Some of the cottagers had a cow, a pig, a horse or a donkey and most of the food required for the sustenance of the animals could be obtained from the common. Heather turf was cut with a special cutter (I have seen this done and helped to do it). Even the dung was collected in the summer and built into neat stacks for the winter fire. Every house had then its bake-oven, and wood collected from the common was used for fuel for the baking. When the common was enclosed the poor people, who perhaps had an animal or two, but paid no rates lost their grazing and other privileges, but received no compensation. Nevertheless in a few years they had accommodated themselves to the changes, and it was from the time that the Acts were applied to Warsash that its development really began.

One of the principal effects of the enclosure of the common was the beginning of the roads as we know them to-day, and having arrived at this point we can now commence our history proper.

The natural starting point is at Warsash Corner. From that point four main roads radiate, corresponding roughly to the four cardinal points of the compass North, South, East and West. They are known as Shore Road, Brook Lane, Titchfield Road, and Newtown Road. We shall consider them in the order named.

SHORE ROAD

Shore Road, as its name indicates leads to the river, and we shall find that in early times this road was to a large extent the centre of life and activity in the district.

The first house on the Shore Road in 1864 was a picturesque old cottage know as Ivy Cottage, deriving its name from the fact that it was almost completely covered with ivy. It had a garden which was separated from the road by wooden palings. This garden contained a fine fig tree, also a large cherry tree overhanging the door near the road; an object of much interest to small boys at a certain season of the year. The cottage was owned by Mr. Richard Bevis, and it was here that the first religious services at Warsash were held. Adjoining the garden was a small shop owned by Miss Emily Bevis. This building was originally built, and for some years used as a Chapel, until it came into the possession of Miss Bevis. Readers of a puritanical turn of mind will regret to hear that in her time it was possible for children to buy sweets at the shop on Sunday, but we are unable to record whether those who did so turned out to be sinners of a deeper dye than the rest of their generation.

By this shop there was a Clap Gate across the road, placed there in order to prevent cattle which were turned out to graze on the common, from straying down to the shore. Just beyond this point was a wheelwright's and carpenter's shop, owned by the father of Miss Bevis, and later used in the same business by her brother, Mr. Owen Bevis. They also had a cattle shed at the back in a small field, and owned another field at Newtown. Almost every day a couple of cows could be seen walking leisurely, as is the manner of cows, up from Newtown to their home, followed by another brother, Mr. Cuthbert Bevis, who, as I remember him, usually wore a very old slouch hat with a hole in the crown, through which a lock of hair protruded and waved fitfully in the breeze.

Continuing down Shore Road for some little distance, which was here bordered by great elms, you next came to a building that was used as a coal store. This belonged to Mr. William Emery, and behind it was the house in which he lived. Next along the road was the garden of the "Shipwrights Arms" public house, and then the public house itself. The landlord at the time I am writing about was a Mr. Ned Budden. In those days the public houses were open all day till 10.30 p.m. and were not generally so well conducted as they are in these modern times. Apparently this house was a particularly noisy one. Complaints were often received that men did not go back to their work in the afternoons, and the noise they made so annoyed the owner of the estate opposite (Mr. Sartoris sen.) that he eventually bought the "Shipwrights Arms" and the blacksmith's shop adjoining, and closed the public house. At the east end of the house, which was a very ancient structure, a modern cottage was built and next door, at the shore end of it, was the blacksmith's forge.

In the year 1870 Mr. Thomas Boyes was the blacksmith, and like the traditional village blacksmith, went on Sunday to the church (he was the sexton and rang the church bell) and not only did he "listen to his daughter's voice, singing in the village choir" but was a notable singer in the choir himself. On the premises occupied by him was a brass plate, belonging to the Sun Insurance Company, and a copy of the first receipt was in his possession, shewing that Widow Chiddell paid the first premium on May 21st 1779, a certain amount for a thatched house, and a smaller amount for a building at the back which was used as a brewery. Mr. C. Boyes, son of Mr. Thomas Boyes, has still these articles in his possession, the receipt being framed in oak taken from the old house.

Next to the blacksmith's shop was another small piece of garden and then two cottages built right on the edge of the road. Between these two cottages doors, which were quite close together, was a boundary stone, and when the boundary was taken, it was necessary to climb over the houses. I remember that they were occupied by Mr. Sweetenham and Mr. Willsher. Beside, and extending behind these cottages was a small estate on which was built a large private house, which was then called Warsash Lodge, or Cottage. General Havelock, of Indian Mutiny fame, lived here for a time, and a road which led from the house to Newtown Road was named after him. Mr. E. Hills, whose name we shall meet again in another connection also lived here. It was owned for some time by Mr. Sartoris, whose daughter, Mrs. Gordon, and family occupied it. It afterwards came into the possession of Mr. G.A. Shenley, who had it very much enlarged. At one time Lord Ellenborough, one time Lord Chief Justice of England, lived there with his wife and sister, and his brother-in-law. Later still it was occupied by Admiral Weymss, First Sea Lord at the Admiralty for some time during the Great War. He changed its name to Mainsail Haul. The boundary of the property continued along the road as far as the shore, and was a high bank, with oak and elm trees growing in it, and surmounted by a high hedge.

This brings us to the shore itself, to which, as it has played an important part in the history of Warsash, I shall have to devote considerable space

On the shores of the Hamble river, in early times, was a flourishing ship-building industry, and of this industry Warsash had its share. In the *Glasgow Herald* of March 1st, 1936, under the heading "Spacious Days", the following notes occur. "The forthcoming launch of H.M.S. Hotspur from the yard of Messrs. Scott's of Greenock, recalls an earlier Hotspur, the first ship of that name in the Royal Navy. She was of 952 tons displacement and was laid down at Warsash on the Southampton Water in August 1807. Three years and two months later she was launched. She had been longer on the stocks than the actual working time involved in building and fitting out the Queen Mary, which has a displacement of 77,000 tons." Things weren't done in such a rush in those days. It is interesting to note that on the shore, halfway between Dock House and the end of the cliff, Mr. James Lock, many years ago, when making an oyster pond, found a number of immense elm timbers embedded in the mud which had obviously formed part of a slipway for the launching of ships. I have been told that the last ship to be built at Warsash on the old slipway was a boom-defence ship for use by the Fleet in the Baltic during the Russian War.

Just in front of where Dock House stands today was formerly a large shed. On the shore side the brickwork reached to the roof, and had an opening with a wooden shutter in the centre of the wall. On the Shore Road side the brickwork of the shed was about four feet high, the upper portion being of weatherboard, very heavily tarred. It had three small span roofs, and was known as the moulding shed. It was in this building that the timbers were specially shaped for ship-building. A little way along the shore, toward the cliff, was a large saw-pit, where the timbers could be sawn.

Between the saw-pit and the slipway was a large patch of grassland, now washed away by the tides. On the spot stood a small cottage where lived Mr. Andrew Haynes, the village blacksmith of those early days. He had a large family and was the last person to live in the cottage. The piece of grassland near the cottage was the usual place for the settlement of quarrels by fighting, after more peaceable ways had failed. I have been told of a small girl coming along the shore from Newtown to attend Miss Swinton's school, standing white and frightened whilst one of these frequent fights were in progress, being afraid to pass; and of a big lad picking her up and taking her past the scene of combat and on to school in the Shrubbery. This was in 1861. In this year 1938 there is no trace of that grassland remaining.

Further along the shore to the North is a good-sized pond known as the fish pond. Originally the banks were built of mud and seaweed. There is some uncertainty about the reason for which it was built. It is stated by some of the older people that it was built as a fish pond either by the monks of Hamble Priory, or those of Titchfield Abbey. The first "hard" for Warsash was near the pond on the South side, but was for many years called Fawley Hard, presumably because many barges were loaded there with corn, to be taken for grinding to the tidal mill at Fawley. It was there that the first coal was unloaded, to be taken up behind the cottage near the pond for Mr. Bevis who sold it, and was there stacked in great heaps under some very large elm trees. I remember talking to a friend somewhat older than myself about the fish pond, and he made the remark, "Why, I've seen live codfish swimming about in the pond." I had seen this myself, but it was so long ago that when I had mentioned it to others, they told me I must have dreamt it. The codfish were brought from the North Sea in well-bottomed ships, and when a customer wanted one Mr. Charlie Gale would catch it for them.

In those days it was not an uncommon sight to see square-rigged vessels with all sails set, going up the river to Bursledon with coal from Sunderland. If there was no wind the men would get into a rowing boat and tow ahead, to keep the ship moving faster than the tide so that she could be steered. It was a great pleasure to a housewife when she could get a set of Sunderland ware, which was a kind of brown glazed earthenware made in six sizes. This was brought from Sunderland by the sailors who manned the colliers and made a little pocket money by selling it.

In the year 1864 there were two firms at Hamble who dealt in shellfish. They owned several vessels that went to places on the coast of Devonshire and Cornwall, to collect the crabs caught locally by the fishermen. They also went to Ireland for lobsters and to France for crayfish and scallops. The crabs, though caught in the west of England, were always known as Hamble crabs. In Warsash at that time lived Mr. James Lock, whose original business was that of rag and bone gatherer. He was evidently a man of keen business instincts for he started to extend by selling fish and meat in a cottage near the shore, and when he received orders for crabs or lobsters he would go to Hamble and buy them at wholesale prices for retail to his customers. He then conceived the idea of getting a boat of his own, but lacked the necessary capital. In pursuance of this idea he found two friends Mr. Birch and Mr. Sims, who were willing to make a venture. The necessary funds were found between them, the ship was bought and the venture proved an immediate success. It was not long before Mr. Lock owned several vessels and built up a thriving business, in which he made use of the old fishpond to keep the fish alive until they were required for sale. The fish crawling about in the pond were always an attraction for visitors.

His ships went as far as the North Sea dredging for oysters on the east side of England, and as far as Stornoway on the west. Many of the crabs were kept in large wooden receptacles known locally as "carbs". They were entered through a lid at the top and were drilled at the sides with holes to allow the free passage of water. They were anchored in the river just off the hard at what was known as the "carb moorings". When the fish were required, the carbs were towed ashore and landed on the hard at high water. When the tide went down they were left high and dry and could be emptied without difficulty.

At that time the nearest railway station was at Fareham, and the transport of baskets and tubs of crabs and lobsters to the station was a big business in the season, to the benefit mostly of those smallholders who lived on the common and had a horse and cart. This trade was mostly done in the summer months in the winter the trade was switched over to oysters and scallops. Even in those days it was possible to glut the market, and I have known of times when the fishermen, who worked the winter trade on the share system, only received ten shillings for as many as a thousand dozen of scallops. This of course is an extreme example, as in general they were able to make a fair living at this trade. When the vessels came back with their cargoes of fish, they were put on the hard at high-water, being kept upright as the tide went down by stout timbers fixed to their sides. This enabled the fish to be cleared right out of the wells, and either stored in the fish pond or sent direct to market. The many holes in the bottom of the ships, which could be seen right through when they were empty, were always a source of puzzlement to visitors, who were at a loss to understand why, with so many holes in them, they did not sink. The ships were, of course, built with two watertight bulkheads, and the holes were essential to keep a circulation of water. When the vessel was in motion, the movement up and down and through the water, kept it pouring in and out of these holes and kept the fish alive. If she became becalmed for any length of time, the fish had to be scooped out of the wells with long poles fitted with an iron hoop and net at the end, and hung round the sides of the ship in large nets until a breeze came and the ship started to move again.

Even when the fish were transferred to the carbs care was necessary. On one occasion after a period of very heavy rain, so much fresh water came down the river from Botley that the crabs began to die, and the carbs had to be hurriedly towed out into Southampton Water.

Mr. Lock used to buy ships of a size suitable for his purpose, haul them up on the old slipway, and employ shipwrights to fit them up for his fish-carrying trade. For special jobs he used to get timber from Wickham. The names of his ships were at one time household words in Warsash, for although several of his captains came from Salcombe in Devon, they brought their wives and families with them and made their homes at Warsash. The crews were nearly all Warsash men. The names of some of his ships were "Stella", "Gem", "Jubilee", "Imogen", "Eudora", "Bonnie Lass", "Harriet" and "Cupid". The sea, as in other places, took her toll both of ships and men. The "Imogen" was lost in the North Sea whilst oyster dredging. Presumably she sank in a gale, for nothing was ever heard of her. The "Bonnie Lass" was lost in Ireland, also the "Harriet". The "Gem" went ashore on a shoal at Spithead, in a tempest of wind and snow. She came off again and made the river, but not until her captain and cabin boy had been drowned.

In the year 1880 a Coastguard Station was built at Newtown to accommodate an officer, eight men, and their families. Prior to this, four families had lived in an old wooden hulk that at one time did duty as guardship off Netley hospital. She was beached for coastguard purposes near the mouth of the river. When the station was built, Mr. James Lock bought the old hulk, had it towed up to Warsash and beached near the old saw pit, made some structural alterations to the interior, named it "Gypsy Queen", and used it for crab and lobster teas in the summer and for dancing in the winter. A big business was done in crab teas and one could see horse-brakes from Portsmouth and Gosport going to the shore nearly every day. As many as 200 people would sometimes visit Warsash for the crab teas in a single day. Naturally, some competition arose and at several of the cottages in Shore Road, notably those of Mr. H. Buckett, Mr. H. Fuger, and Mr. H. Butcher, as well as at the "Rising Sun" public house, crab teas could be obtained. The old "Gypsy Queen" was eventually broken up and the villagers purchased her timbers for sawing up in chunks to burn. By reason of the tar with which they were impregnated they burnt very fiercely.

The "Rising Sun" faces the shore and stands on the North side of the road. Since it faces West and the rising sun never shines on it, one wonders what humorist gave it that name. It is so near the beach that very high tides reach the wall of the house, and have been known to flood the cellars. A former landlord once shewed me a fine sketch of the "Rising Sun" made about the year 1869 when I first saw it.

There was a front entrance through a porch, rather to one side of the building, the tap room was between this and the Shore Road and was lighted by one window. On the other side were three windows, which lighted the hotel portion and the private rooms. There were the same number of windows on the next storey, and along the eaves of the roof was a wide signboard bearing the name Sun Hotel. This appears to have been the original name. When it was changed to *Rising Sun* I do not know. A low paling ran along the whole length of the building with exception of the width of the porch, and connected with it was a strong seat on which customers and others could sit and see all that was going on on the shore or in the river opposite.

I had the pleasure of sitting on that seat with old Sam Emery amongst others. He was then nearly 90 years of age, almost blind, and his hair was very white. He would talk to me of the olden days and of the alterations and changes that the years had brought. He lived in an old cottage on the edge of the common at the bottom of Havelock Road. Mr. George Hewett was the name of the landlord of the inn. He used to sell tea in packets that had been brought by his brother from India. There were stables and a yard at the back with an entrance from Shore Road, and beyond the stables a piece of ground where the now practically extinct game of Quoits used to be played.

A little farther along the shore stood a flagstaff and a little farther still a footpath leading up through the "Shrubbery" at the back of the houses on this side of Shore Road, joining the road halfway up the hill. There was a piece of waste land on the shore here, and on this I once saw a "cheapjack" with his van. To advertise his goods he was offering a prize to anyone who could eat a boiling hot plum pudding with his hands tied behind him. Amongst the competitors, who numbered four, was a shepherd named Jack King. The puddings were turned out of the basins in front of the men; the word to go was given, and Jack King, having a somewhat original notion about how to win, bashed the pudding flat with his forehead. He won the match to the accompaniment of loud cheers, the others being mostly unable to eat for laughing, but not without considerable detriment to the skin of his forehead.

A cottage stood beyond this land, inhabited by Mr. Bevis, and behind it was kept a large heap of coal, which had only been in use in the village for a few years. Mr. Sartoris owned the land and cottage, and later turned the cottage into a yacht store. Later still, Mr. G.A. Shenley removed the first floor and roof, because it obstructed his view of the river from Warsash House. From this cottage to the beginning of Passage Lane there was a low bank and some fine elm trees. Passage Lane branched off to the right and joined the Shore Road about halfway up the hill, at the same point as the footpath through the Shrubbery. About the centre of the triangle formed by Passage Lane, the Shore, and Shore Road, there was a well which supplied the cottages, and also the shipping which sailed from Warsash, with water. There were a number of fishermen, some of whom lived in the cottages by the shore. Some of the fish they caught were sold at the large houses in the district, but the bigger part went to Southampton or Portsmouth. In the case of the smaller craft, each fisherman owned his own boat and gear.

In some of the larger vessels several men were employed, usually four, and in the winter time spratting was a flourishing industry. The boats were worked on the share system, the owner taking two shares for supplying ship and nets, and the men one share each. The captain, where he was not the owner himself, usually got a small bonus. In the year 1874 and a year or two later, great quantities of sprats were caught and the market could not absorb them. They were sold to the farmers and smallholders at sixpence a bushel for manure After this the industry gradually declined and eventually it completely died out. Some of the vessels rotted in their berths on the mud, and at low tide even today some of their timbers may be seen sticking out. Amongst the vessels used for spratting were "Vulcan", belonging to Mr. James Dimmick, "Martha", to Mr. Hiram Dimmick, "Gnome" to Mr. H. Buckett, and "Albion" to Mr. Bob Silvester. The "Albion" was known locally as the "training ship" as Mr. Bob Silvester used to get young lads from the farms as well as sons of the older fishermen, and train them for the sea. This vessel was also employed in bringing cider from Devonshire to Southampton.

Another large vessel that paid occasional visits to Hamble river was a topsail-yard schooner named the "Commodore". She belonged to Captain Sam Cutt, who came from Goole, in Yorkshire. He used to trade from various ports round the coast and across to France and Holland. Eventually he had the misfortune to lose his ship by shipwreck on the Cornish coast. He settled down in Warsash and opened a general shop in Newtown Road, but his heart was always at sea, and he had two or three small sailing boats, one of which was named "Commodore" after his old schooner, and about these boats he used to spend most of his spare time. Another boat well known at Warsash was a flat-bottomed sailing barge named "Robert and Sarah" belonging to Mr. Robert Budden. This barge was sometimes employed to bring street refuse from Portsmouth and Southampton. There was another well known vessel named "Lucretia", owned by Captain French, which traded around the coast and frequently visited Warsash; and another large barge called "Harriet" was often in and out of the river. The chemical factory at Newtown (to which we shall come later) provided a good deal of business for shipping. Amongst other things wood was brought from Beaulieu to make charcoal.

We must now leave the shore and proceed back up the hill along Shore Road. After leaving the "Rising Sun" there are a number of cottages on the left side of the road, to which consideration must be given. First we find three cottages built about 1864, and one house built partly of wood with four steps leading up to the ground floor. Mr. Thomas Bevis, who lived there, used to keep a monkey and I and other small boys used to go during the dinner-hour from school, to watch the antics of the little beast. Darwin's "missing link" was at that time a frequent topic of conversation among the older people but the interest of the boys and girls (all of whom possess a great deal of natural curiosity) was probably due to the strange antics and expressions of the animal, and not from any desire to investigate the scientific problem. Another cottage further up the hill was a very strongly built old place, constructed of brick and stone, with very large fireplaces, and beams of oak made intensely hard by age. In my opinion this house was built about the same time as the "Shipwrights Arms" and as it had a tiled roof and was in its day a superior class of building, it is possible that it belonged to or was occupied by the owner or overseer of the shipbuilding yard on the shore. There is evidence that the house stood quite alone and must have been built before 1807. There is an interesting story of this house connecting it with smuggling. Some years ago it became necessary to take down a part of one of the bedroom ceilings and to the workmen's surprise on entering the roof, it was found to contain a large quantity of contraband, which had at some time been secreted there, and for some reason or other had never been removed. Mr. Harry Buckett and his descendants have been the occupants of this house for many years. There are two cottages now attached to this one, but they were probably built some years after the first. There was an open space next to Mr. Buckett's cottage where later a coalstore was erected. Between this and the end of Passage Lane was a low bank behind which was the upper part of the Shrubbery. There were here a good number of trees with a fair amount of open space between. This was open to the public though actually a part of the Warsash House estate.

It was among these trees that the Warsash and District Annual Fair was held, usually in February. Mr. "Jimmy" Burchell, a notable character, who was a travelling showman, was always there on these occasions, and his collection of amusements provided the chief attraction. Among other things there was a shooting gallery, coconut shies, and a dressed-up guy with a pipe in its mouth, at which short sticks were thrown with the object of smashing the pipe. It was found that the young men in their excitement got so uncertain in their aim that the sticks became dangerous, and later, wooden balls were substituted for them. "Jimmy" provided his own music. He had an instrument constructed of a number of reed pipes of different lengths and attached to a piece of wood about a foot long. This piece of wood he used to stick down inside his coat, which was tightly buttoned across his chest, bringing the ends of the reeds level with his mouth, with which he used to blow into them. It was quite a sight to see his head wagging from side to side as his mouth travelled up and down the reeds at an incredible rate. He had a drum in front of him, which he beat loudly as an accompaniment, and on a still evening the sound of pipes and drum could be heard all over the village. He was a clever performer with the shadograph and no one who had seen it would be likely to forget "The bridge is broke and I've got to mend it, Fol de riddle I doh, fol de riddle a." He also ran a peep show of "Battles in France", "Landscapes", Beautiful Women", interspersed with a few comic pictures. Mrs. Burchell made a much appreciated brand of "home-made rock" which was eagerly bought up by young people and not a few of the older ones. Mrs. Burchell was a native of Warsash, her father being the one-time blacksmith Andrew Haynes. Jimmy usually made a three or four days stay at Warsash. After his death his eldest son Jim carried on the business in a modernised form, but soon ceased to visit Warsash.

Leaving the Shrubbery and proceeding up the hill, we skirt the border of the Warsash House estate, in this part a high bank covered with shrubs, on past the entrance to the house itself and then to four cottages in one block which were occupied by workmen employed on the estate. We then come to some large doors, being the back entrance to Warsash House and the stables, then a further high bank with some large elm trees and thus finish our survey of Shore Road and arrive back at the Corner.

BROOK LANE

We now commence our survey of the second of the roads radiating from Warsash Corner. As we come up the Shore Road we turn left at the corner into Brook Lane. This was in early days, the main road out of Warsash. It runs to Park Gate where it connects with the Portsmouth-Southampton road.

For some little distance as we proceed up the lane, it is the boundary of the Warsash House estate and it will perhaps be convenient if we now deal with that house, as it has had a considerable bearing on the life and development of Warsash, and thus has a large claim on our interest. In the year 1854 Warsash House was occupied by Colonel Swinton and his daughter, Miss Caroline Swinton. With Miss Swinton's work in Warsash I shall deal later, in the next section of this history. The house was not a very large one and was probably in its original form a farmhouse of the better class, but many alterations and additions were made to it in the course of its existence.

After Colonel Swinton, Mr. Sartoris and his wife came to Warsash House and as it was not large enough for their requirements, additions in the Italian style were built on at each end and another floor added. Mr. Sartoris was an artist and built a large studio on the North side of the house. Mrs Sartoris was a singer in grand opera. They had two sons and a daughter in family and during their occupation they entertained many visitors of social eminence and distinguished in art and literature. Edward the Seventh stayed there when he was Prince of Wales; Sir Frederick Leighton, president of the Royal Academy, also paid several visits. One of the sons, Mr. Algernon Sartoris, visited America and brought back as his bride Miss Nellie Grant, daughter of President and Mrs. Grant, who afterwards came and stayed at Warsash House as guests. As General Grant he commanded the victorious Northern armies in the American civil war. I must here digress a little in order to recount a thrilling experience of my own. At the time I was garden boy on the estate and everybody with the exception of the second gardener, Mr. George Pedrick, and myself, had gone to a shooting party at Locks Heath, where he (Mr. Sartoris) rented the shooting rights from Mr. Quintin Hogg. While they were away a telegram came to the house asking Mr. Sartoris to meet someone in London, and I went post-haste to Locks Heath in a pony and cart to deliver it; and brought him back to the house to prepare for his journey. Now he had brought back from America a fast-trotting horse and a contraption known as a "buggey", which was little more than a framework on wheels with a cane seat just large enough to accommodate the driver. Whilst he was getting ready, Pedrick and I got out the horse and buggey. Neither he nor I had had anything to do with it previously. The nearest railway station was Fareham, and he was going to drive there. But who was going to bring the vehicle back? Mr. Algernon got into the seat and shouted "Get up, boy!" I stood aghast, but was told to stand on the back axle, put my arms round his waist, and *hold on*. Pedrick led the horse out through the big doors into the road, let go; and before I had properly recovered we were in Fareham. Just a trot, but what a trot! I got down and went to the horse's head, Mr. Algernon went into the station and found that he was in time for his train. He then came back and told me to drive home quietly.

I though, "Now, my beauty, you can walk all the way home." I turned the horse round in the yard with all the cabmen watching me (they had seen it before) and quite a little crowd collected to see me off; a small boy, on four wheels and a framework, and the reputed fastest horse in the country. A man stepped up and held the horse while I got seated and took the reins, which had special loops in order to give a good grip; and we started. From Fareham station there is a hairpin bend to get into the Titchfield Road and it is a bit steep at the corner. The buggey must have pushed against the horse for he moved a little faster; I pulled gently on the reins, and that did it. There was fortunately but little traffic. I had just time to indulge in a little worry about how I was going to get round the bend in Titchfield, before finding that I was round it and in the square, without altering the pull on either hand. Mr. Jim Bungey told me afterward that the horse was going all out, and that I was very white. Almost before I realised it, we were at Warsash, outside the door leading to the stables where the horse stopped so suddenly that he almost threw me off.

In the grounds of Warsash House there was a carriage drive of some length, and Mr. Sartoris frequently hired a photographer to take pictures of himself, driving the trotter.

One of his favourite amusements was fishing with a net known as a trammel. He would employ Mr. Henry Moody and his son Walter, with their big rowing boat "Double Ration" to take them out. Mr. John West usually accompanied them on these expeditions. Trammel fishing is done at night, and they usually fished in a large bay in the Solent just below Calshot, about midnight. I once accompanied them, and Mr. Sartoris, noticing that I was an abstainer from strong drink, told the men to put me overboard or they would catch no fish. I doubt if it was a case of cause and effect, but they did *not* put me overboard, and they certainly caught very little fish on that occasion.

Mrs. Sartoris was an exceedingly nice lady, and was considered to be a beauty. I often saw her about the garden. At one time when she was recovering from an illness it was my job to take her out in a donkey-shay. She was very fond of the quiet lanes and woods. One pleasant walk in particular went through Brook Avenue woods to a meadow on the shore, ending at Cobbett's Creek. In the centre of this wood was a large sand pit; Mrs. Sartoris had been told that it had been used by smugglers, and one day when we were there she asked me if I knew anything about it. I was able to tell her that my mother, who was born and brought up at Great Brook, which could be seen through the trees, had several times seen the pit full of contraband goods; and had told me who had shares in it, and how the goods were disposed of.

Changes took place on the Warsash House estate as the years passed. Mr. Sartoris built a model farm in Brook Lane, where he kept fine Alderney cows. Mr. William Barry was the cowman. The old farm was over against the shore, behind the new one, and years before was worked by Mr. Emery. I remember that farm well, because the only hornets' nest that I ever saw was in the granary roof. In 1874, in the middle of the field next to the model farm, Mr. Algernon Sartoris had a cricket pitch made, and it was played on for years. I was once selected to play on the side of Mr. Sartoris, but I fear, only as a stop-gap.

A few years later Mr. G.A. Shenley came to Warsash House, and after a time made considerable alterations to it. He had the chimneys rebuilt with tiled roofs on each, and replaced the slated roof with Roman tiles, thus giving the house a slightly foreign appearance. He also made alterations to the front entrance by

Warsash House

Shore Road, Warsash

The Rising Sun, Warsash

Brook Farm, Warsash

Cross Roads, Warsash

Newtown Road, Warsash

Thornton Avenue, Warsash

The Sun Hotel, Warsash

Fleet End

Hook Church

The Newbury Home and Workshop

The Newbury Family

building a massive stone doorway. He had a Greek fireplace put in the hall, and in the frieze above, which was of stone and about a foot wide, was carved a boar-hunting scene which was a very fine piece of work. He also had a fine small organ installed which was electrically blown, and is now at St. Mary's Church at Hook. Mr. and Mrs. Shenley usually spent the winter in Albania hunting wild boars. Near the Corner, he built a very fine garage and electric lighting plant, also a water-tower on which was a clock whose bells struck the hours in nautical fashion. He possessed a fine steam-yacht named "Triad" which had her moorings in the Hamble river opposite the estate and in her he made several voyages to the Mediterranean, Mr. J.R. Dickinson being the navigator.

After Mr. Shenley, Mr. Graham White occupied the house for a few years, and later it was acquired by Lord and Lady Stalbridge. The estate was bought by a land company in 1934 for development and in 1937 Warsash House was pulled down and cleared right away.

Proceeding further along Brook Lane we pass what was formerly known as Red House, in which the bailiff of the Warsash House estate used to live, and then to Great Brook farm, a fine old house, which has now been turned into a modern dwelling and considerably altered. Opposite this house Greenaways Lane turns off to the right.

Greenaways Lane, like all the old roads, and some of the new ones, was originally a cart-track made by the passage of carts and waggons. It was designed to be about eight foot wide, but as the carts went from side to side to avoid deep potholes, the actual width was about fifteen feet, varying, of course, in places. By the side of, and sometimes on the track itself, grew oak, ash, shrubs and brambles, and in many places great clumps of furze. It was here in 1871 that I saw old Mark Hill, the official roadman, working. His job was to form a water-table and to straighten up the road so that the water could get away. Some of the oak and other growths had to be grubbed out, and the gravelly soil was put into the potholes. In November patches of gravel were put on, but the sort of gravel then used had no binding properties and the surface soon became very loose. For many years, all roads both old and new, were treated in this fashion. Until comparatively recent years there were only four cottages in this lane: three in a block and one standing with its end to the road. They are called Brook Cottages. Near these cottages a stream crosses the road. This stream comes down through the meadow on one side and continues on through Dibles Bottom, finally ending in Hook Lake. A public footpath runs by its side for a large part of its course, beginning at Dibles Bottom, crossing the Warsash-Titchfield road and Greenaways Lane and proceeding up through the long meadows and Littlewood copse to Brook Lane. On a waste piece of land in Greenaways Lane the gypsies had a camp site where they used to, and still camp, sometimes for weeks. I believe their names were Lee, Stanley and Bowers, the true gypsy tribe. Greenaways Lane joins the Warsash-Titchfield road at the farther end.

A little further up Brook Lane there is a footpath on the right, with a stile at either end, joining Brook Lane with Greenaways Lane. A little further still, and on the left we reach Brook Farm, near where the brook crosses the road, and by this brook on the left is the entrance to a narrow road leading down to the shore and known as Brook Avenue. This was at one time used as a direct road from Hamble to Titchfield, the ferry from Hamble landing passengers at the bottom of the road. It has long fallen into disuse except as a means of access to those houses built upon it, and as an occasional Sunday afternoon walk. At the bottom of the lane a footpath runs along the bank, leading on the left to Warsash shore, and on the right to Swanwick shore and Bursledon.

A few yards farther on we come to a point where five roads meet. On the extreme left is a new road which was made when the property in that direction was developed, and which curves round at the bottom to join with Brook Avenue. Next to it there is a road bearing slightly to the left out of Brook Lane. This is Barnes Lane. In early days this lane dwindled to a footpath through Winnards Copse, and then proceeded across the common to Sarisbury as a cart track. The old main road goes straight on to Park Gate and this was at one time actually the main road out of Warsash. On the right is a rough road called Peters Road, which led across the common to Locks Farm.

I used sometimes to take Mrs. Sartoris along this road to the highest point of the common, for the sake of the view which on a clear day was a very lovely one. There was a clear space there, just behind where the house known as the Flagstaff now stands, and from there one could see the Isle of Wight, the Solent, Southampton Water, a little of Hamble river and a part of Hill Head. In August the racing yachts with their lovely snow-white canvas could be seen racing at Cowes, and sailing ships of all descriptions going about their lawful occasions. There were very few steamers in those days. A few years later a German consul, Mr. Keller, saw the place and when Mr. Quintin Hogg, to whom the common belonged, put it on the market, Mr. Keller bought this spot and built the Flagstaff on it. He actually had by the house a very high flagstaff, on which both the Union Jack and the German flag were flown every day.

In early days the first bread delivered to Warsash came from Sarisbury from Mr. W.A. Newbury's shop and bakery on the Green. Previous to this the inhabitants baked their own bread, but when the common was shared out the difficulty in obtaining fuel became so great that this had to be given up, and the way was open for the entrance of the bakery trade. Competition, of course, soon arose, and the next to deliver bread in Warsash was Mr. F. King, of Titchfield. About 1869 the first bakery in Warsash itself was established by Mr. E. Pounsett at Dibles. He delivered round Warsash in the mornings, and Mrs. Pounsett delivered at Sarisbury in the afternoons, thus carrying the war into the enemy's camp after the time-honoured custom. A great deal of comment was made on the taste of the bakers' bread, and it was particularly noted that it got stale very quickly, whereas home-baked bread was considered good at a week old. This ends our survey of Brook Lane.

TITCHFIELD ROAD

From Warsash Corner, going in an easterly direction, we proceed along the road leading to Titchfield, Fleetend, and Hook. For some little distance along the left there was a high bank, covered with oak, ash, holly and brambles, all growing wild as was the custom of boundary hedges before the common enclosure. This wild growth often extended into the field for a rod or more. After the enclosure the quick hedge came almost immediately into use, and almost without exception every quick hedge that may now be seen growing was planted before 1870.

On the right, and almost on the corner stands the house known as Binfield. Miss Caroline Swinton, to whom I referred earlier, owned the piece of land on which this was built. She had a very keen interest in the education of the young, and here she built a school, and rooms over it in which she lived. At a later date she built Binfield in which she lived till the time of her death. On Sunday the premises were used for religious services under the auspices of the Plymouth Brethren, of which sect she was a devoted adherent. I went to that school in 1869, and remember that on two occasions a gentleman came to the school with a large roll of canvas on which was painted a continuous series of pictures in colours, explanatory of the lecture which he had come to deliver. It took two strong boys, one to unroll and the other to roll up the canvas, as the picture was of considerable length. We knew it as a "Panorama" and enjoyed it immensely. Mr. William Waight and Miss Martell were the head teachers.

The scholars were required to pay twopence per week toward cost of their education. With the advent of free education the school was closed. There was also a girls school in the woods near Hook, under the patronage of the Hornby family, of which Miss Shorten was the mistress. At times when a special visitor came to Warsash school, Miss Shorten's girls would come over to hear the lecture. There was no playground for the children until a few years before the school was closed. They then played in the road, which in those days was quite a safe thing to do; but eventually Miss Swinton bought a plot of land on the Corner, from Mr. Bevis, the greater part of which was turned into a playground.

Next to the school was a plot of land apportioned by the Titchfield Vestry to be used as "allotments for ever" for the use of cottagers whose cottages lacked sufficient ground for a garden. After St. Mary's church was built in 1871, and a new parish formed called Hook-with-Warsash; these allotments were invested in the Churchwardens of St. Mary's. Later still, when Parish Councils came into being, the Charity Commissioners took them over. When the piece of land was first marked off, Mr. William Barry was one of the men who planted the quick hedge on its four sides. Similar arrangements for allotments were made at Hunts Pond Road, at Sarisbury behind the vicarage, and at Crofton. The next piece of land was a narrow strip, running back a long way, in a line with Newtown Road to the Cutting. This land was made over to Mr. George Gray, who a few years later made up his mind to sell it in plots. From the main road a cart track about 15 feet wide was marked out the whole length of the field, and then various parts were sold. Here Mr. James Moody bought the first plot and built a house.

Mr. James Lock bought a large part of the field, and as he had also bought the buildings which had been used as a chemical works (to which I shall refer later) he used the bricks and other materials for building houses Mr. C.J. Newbury and others also built houses there, using material from the same source. This cart track is now part of Osborn Road. Later, when the common next to it was put up for sale, a fifteen feet wide strip of the common was given and included in the road. There was some years between the making of the two roads, which gives us a case of a private road being made in two halves.

Just above this on the main road was a five-barred gate, and the road was carried over a brick culvert through which ran, at times, quite a lot of water. It was a favourite amusement of most boys and some girls to crawl through the culvert, which was only fourteen inches wide. A few years later inside the gate a Reading Room was built. Mr. Sartoris, who had bought the field from Quintin Hogg, Esq., gave the land, and lent £100 to help the funds for building.

A little farther up the road, on the right, we come to a wide ornamental gate with iron posts to match; a small gate on one side and a dummy gate on the other. This was the entrance to a private road to Hook House. When the gate was set up, elm trees were planted at intervals on both sides of the raod, interspersed with clumps of shrubs. These extended across the common to the old Hook Lodge. The original idea was to form a fine avenue, but the young trees were neglected and only a few near the Warsash end of the road survived for a few years. At this end of the road another lodge was built just inside the iron gate by Arthur Hornby, Esq., son of William Hornby, Esq., in 1871. Here lived Mr. Randall, formerly the family butler of the Hornbys. At the Hook end of the road at this time St. Mary's Church was being built. It was constructed of Swanage stone. The foundation stone was laid in 1870 and forms the plinth at the East end of the church. On it are the letters G.R. in lead. The stone was laid by Thomas Robinson, Esq., brother-in-law to Arthur Hornby, who built the church and endowed it. In the North-east side of the church is a stained glass window to the memory of Thomas Robinson, and a brass in memory of Thomas Boyes, the first sexton. He held that office for twenty years and also served as church warden. The church was opened in 1871 and called St. Mary's. In 1872 the ecclesiastical parish was called Hook-with-Warsash. A fine vicarage was built near the church, and the first vicar was Rev. John Gamon. A stone wall encircles the church and graveyard, which is reached by a fine oak lych-gate.

Across the road is the school and the schoolmaster's house. Mr. Arthur Hornby had intended to build the church on the old estate at Hook, in front of the wheelwright's shop, but it was pointed out to him that a large majority of the people in the district lived at Warsash, so he finally decided to build it in its present position. The road from the iron gate to the church was then called Church Road.

A little farther up the main road from the iron gate we come to a fork in the road. For the present we will take the left fork, leading by the Independent Chapel.

The Independent Chapel was built in a field owned by Mr. James Gray, and tilled by Mr. Peter Dimmick, Jun., who was also the carrier to Southampton three times a week. Mr. James Gray gave the land for the erection of the chapel, the foundation stone of which was laid on July 22nd 1854. The chapel had originally only one door, which led into it directly from the road. The back half of the interior was fitted with seats that had upright backs about four feet high. The remaining seats had low backs. There was a gallery over the entrance door, facing the pulpit, where the choir used to sit, the choirmaster starting the tunes after getting the pitch from a tuning fork. Additions and alterations were made to the chapel, and in 1889 a new chapel was opened by the side of the old one, which was then used as a Sunday School It is notable that in modern years this Sunday School has won the challenge shield for scripture knowledge oftener than any school in England. In the triangle of land almost opposite the chapel, formed by the junction of the two roads, Mrs. Edwards built a general shop.

Proceeding along the road on which the chapel stands, we come shortly to Yew Tree Farm, with its old tree, and double-tenement house open to the farmyard. There were the usual stables and carthouse, and a large barn built end-on to the road. As a small boy I have helped to tread down the corn in the mow, and I have also seen this done by ponies. The reason for so much treading down was that when threshing was done by the flail (a flail is two sticks fastened together with strips of leather), two men would stand facing each other on the barn floor, each swinging his flail around his head and bringing it down on the ears of corn with great force. The men would be at this work all the winter, and it was therefore necessary to get as much corn as possible into the barn. Incidentally, when the mow was full, the ponies were slid down on a quantity of straw. The last time I saw threshing being done by flail was in the Tudor barn at Great Brook in 1870.

At Yew Tree, I remember two occasions when the chapel people had their annual tea in the barn. It was lent to them for that purpose, the time being just before harvest, when the barn was empty. When the tables were set, just above them was the under side of the roof, and it has been related that on one occasion, just as the people were about to commence tea, a rat jumped down and ran along the table amongst the provisions, to the great consternation of those present. This barn was then the only building large enough to accommodate a considerable number of people. Later, after the high seats had been removed from the chapel the teas were held there. While they were being held in the barn, people used to come from Sarisbury, Titchfield, Fareham, and even as far as Gosport in order to attend them. Just below the barn we come to a square modern cottage in which for many years lived the shepherd of this farm, Mr. Weeks and his son Tom. Farther down the hill was an old cottage where Mrs. Gregory lived and kept a general shop. A cow-house and several pigstys were close by.

Mrs. Gregory later disposed of this property to a Mr. and Mrs. Cox, who possessed a remarkable parrot, who was able to give quite a good rendering, more or less in tune, if a bit raucous, of the first line of the chorus of a popular hymn of those days: "Oh, that will be joyful." Opposite the barn, on the other side of the road, was a meadow belonging to the farm. A stream runs along the bottom, crossing the road through a culvert. Along this stream, about halfway to Dibles, was a square brick pit built across the stream, so that by dropping a hatch the pit would be filled with water about three feet deep. This was used for washing the sheep. In those times every farmer had a number of sheep, the number varying according to the acreage of the farm. About May the sheep would be brought to the meadow, and quite large lumps of mud and clay, which had accumulated during the winter, could be seen sticking to the wool. Now that the time had come for the sheep to be sheared, as much as possible of this dirt had to be cleaned off, as it would materially decrease the value of the wool. Now, in 1938, very little of the foundation of this pit is left.

If we now go back to the road and stand on the arch over the stream, looking up the footpath, we see on the right a very old thatched cottage. It has been called Shepherds Cottage for many years. A man used to live there named Jim Crockford, who made the strong reed baskets that farm labourers used to buy for carrying food and drink. When I first remember this cottage, all around, under the eaves of the thatch, were bundles of reeds hung there to dry. These reeds were cut in Hook Lake.

If we now continue along the main road, we shall shortly pass the end of Greenaways Lane, and a little farther on, on the left, we see Upper Brook Farm. I should like to describe here what I saw on a piece of waste land by the side of the road just before reaching the farm. This was in 1870/1 when Upper Brook and Ireland Farms were worked together. They were owned by Mr. George Gray, of Fishhouse (now known as Solent Court), Hook. On this piece of road was an immense heap of manure brought from the farmyard. When making this heap, the head carter would stay on it and tip the loads. A boy with a trace-horse used to help the cart-horse draw the load up and on over the heap after tipping. When the time came to take it to the fields a hay-cutting knife was used to cut it out, to make it easier to load the carts. I have written these details to show the difference that has taken place in the manner of farming. A great deal of guano was used, scraped off the rocks of some desolate island and brought hundreds of miles by sea. It was considered good, but the men handling it took its stench home to the cottages, no matter what care they took to prevent it. Mark Hill, whom I have mentioned before, was roadman at this time, and when he had quartered the road up to this heap of manure, the farmer had orders to remove it, and after a good deal of grumbling it was cleared away.

Upper Brook Farm is on the left of the road as we go in the direction of Titchfield, and was a very fine house in those times. The front door was in the middle, there were windows each side, and a bent coloured glass veranda the whole length of the front. A wide path ran from the door to the road, and near the house was a narrow lawn with flower beds. Rambler roses were trained round the veranda supports. After the lawn was a dwarf hedge, and the remainder formed a vegetable garden with fruit trees

Near the gate was a Yucca tree with its very high stalk of flowers. A wall divided the garden from the farmyard and behind the yard was the back way into the house. Near the house was a barn, used for the storage and preparation of foodstuff for the cattle. At the end of the barn was the stable for the cart-horses, and at the side of this yard the gate opening into the rick-yard.

Beyond this gate were the cowsheds and a stable for a nag or other horse; and between this and the road was a very large barn. Between the barn and the yard gate, opening on to the public road, was a large thatched shed, used in the winter as a shelter for the fattening cattle. Every farm for miles around had a number of Red Devons for fattening purposes. Next along the road, behind some fine elm trees, was a large granary, resting on the usual coped stones. Now we come to a block of sheds made of timber, with large double doors opening on to the road. The backs of these sheds were open, and they were thatched with reeds from Hook Lake. The first part of the shed was used for waggons, carts and farm implements.

Mr. George Gray owned a set of thrashing tackle, as it was then called. One of the sheds held the drums, another the straw-carrier. The engine was just a firebox, boiler, and flywheel driven by cranks. It had a very tall chimney which was laid down when not in use. The engine, drum and carrier was drawn from farm to farm by four horses. William Whale was the engine driver and general mechanic of the farm. A new cottage was built opposite these sheds for the head carter, Mr. William Barton.

The remainder of the road to Lane End was about a quarter of a mile, and ran between fields. At this point the road which we know as Titchfield Road became nothing more than a cart track. At Lane End a culvert was put in and it was here that one crossed the footpath from Brook Lane to Narrow Bridge. From this point it was all common. The track carried on past Jolly's Field until it arrived at the point where Fleetend Road branches off to the right. Here it crossed the stream and continued on across the common to what we know as Doctor's Corner, and from thence on to Park Gate by what is now Locks Road. Locks Road runs in an almost straight line to Park Gate where it joins the South-ampton-Portsmouth road. A little way up the road we pass Locks Farm and Cawtes Farm and just beyond here a new road was made, with a brick culvert to carry it across the stream, and known as Church Road. This joins up with Hunts Pond Road at the further end. The farmers around Abshot, Hook and Chilling used Abshot Road and Hunts Pond Road to get to Botley and Southampton, as though an old road, it was in very good condition.

It must be remembered in writing of these tracks that they were not by any means straight, and it was only when the roads were made up, and culverts put in, that they were straightened up and put into their present position.

At Doctor's Corner is another track bearing to the right, and leading to Titchfield. A little further along this track, at the bottom of the hill, is a rather large stream, which before the common was enclosed and a special brick arch put in to carry the road, was for the greater part of the year difficult to cross. I asked an old lady who used to go that way to attend school at Titchfield, about this stream and she told me that while horses and carts could get through with some difficulty, it was necessary for pedestrians who wished to cross it to go further up the stream where it was narrower. This was about 1861.

Still following the track we come at some little distance to Abshot Road. This road begins at Abshot House, passes Abshot Farm and pond, and continues across the Warsash-Titchfield road on up the common to Hunts Pond Road, at a point near Course House. Continuing on the main road, the common still extended to the left, but further along the track, on the right between a field and a copse, was a gate across the road. This is Hook Gate and is the beginning of the road leading through Hook to Hook House and on to the shore, at Chilling and Brownwich.

Just beyond this, down the hill, is the beginning of Hunts Pond Road, and near this is a stream called the Sluice. Over this are two culverts, one on top of the other. The first was put in in very early days, and the second after the common was enclosed.

At the top of the hill on the right is a lane leading to Brownwich and the shore; and across the road was a gate called Pound Gate, which served the same purpose as the Clap gate at Warsash Corner. On the left is the old cattle "pound". Beyond this the road continues to Titchfield.

Hunts Pond Road, which was a good old road going from the Sluice to Park Gate, follows the old common boundary nearly all the way.

This completes our survey of Titchfield Road, and we must now return to Warsash Corner to commence the survey of the last on our list, Newtown Road.

NEWTOWN ROAD

The Newtown Road runs from Warsash Corner to Newtown. As far as the Cutting it is one of the newer roads from there on is the old road which has been in use for hundreds of years. This piece of road has never been taken over by the authorities, and is still in a rough state. I am unable to state why this should be so. On the right after leaving the Corner is Havelock Road to which we have made previous reference.

Some way down the road, on the left, is a house now named "Dingle", Here was the first Warsash Post Office. The Postmaster, Mr. Baker, and his daughter lived there. In 1869 we were under the Fareham post office, and the letters for Warsash came through

Titchfield. We had no regular postman at that time. The man who brought the letters, and whom I remember quite well, was Mr. Hewlett. He was very deaf, and drove a mule in his cart. He used to bring the letters from Titchfield to "Dingle" for Mr. Baker to deliver. Mr. Baker could not read so his daughter Alice used to put the letters into different pockets for various people, and tell her father to whom the letters in the different pockets were to be given. Mr. Hewlett was sometimes asked for letters on his way to Warsash, and if he was in a good humour he would hand over any that were addressed to you. If he was not in a good humour he would tell you that the letter would be delivered at your house some time during the day. This I know to be a fact because my grandmother occasionally received letters from the Cape of Good Hope, and this really happened a few times when he was met and asked for letters.

The Cutting turns off to the right a little way down the road and formerly led to the chemical works near the shore. These chemical works need a detailed description, as at one time they made a great deal of difference, directly and indirectly to the life of Warsash. They were started about 1864 by Mr. E. Hill, who came from Sussex, and brought several families with him, amongst whom were Mr. and Mrs. Gale. Mr. Gale was the general foreman and lived in a cottage in the works. The leading bricklayer was Mr. Carter, who lived in Warsash with his wife and family. The buildings were built on and around the old salterns. I must here digress for a minute or two to tell you of these salterns. The earliest information we have about Newtown is that salt was collected there by Mr. James Hewett in what were called urns. Hence the name "salterns". These urns were large shallow bays on the shore of the Hamble river where the water was let in at high tide, and then allowed to evaporate, the salt being afterward collected for sale. To go back to the chemical factory, I will describe the buildings as I saw them in 1869.

For the chemical processes there were several long sheds, built side by side, containing wooden and iron vats, both large and small. In some of these sheds were large cylinders in which wood was placed. A fire was then made in the furnace underneath, and the chemicals in the wood were thus extracted, the residue being charcoal, which was used for another purpose at the other end of the factory. In some of the vats were vitriol, and other chemicals. In order to allow the men to do the necessary work, planks were put across these vats, and on one occasion a plank slipped, and the man who was testing the boiling liquid fell in and lost his life. His name was George Pearce. He was married and had three children, and was a splendid fellow, much liked in the village.

In those days, Warsash had its company of Mummers, who used at Christmas time to give a kind of play at various places in the district, often in the high road. The parts were made into a kind of doggerel verse and the main theme might be described in the words used by one of the Mummers.

'In comes I, Old Father Christmas, welcome or welcome not.
I hope Old Father Christmas will never be forgot."

George Pearce always took the part of the doctor. He was only 20 when he died. Mr. William Hewett and Mr. Tom Fuger witnessed the accident.

The factory gave employment to a good number of men. The various sheds covered a large space, and there were large stacks of timber cut into about four feet lengths. The bricks used to build the sheds came from various places, some from as far as Beaulieu, and a good many were made on the place, the clay being taken out of the hill behind Mr. Gale's cottage, and burnt in clamps. Portland cement was also made here by Messrs. Hooper and Ashby, of Southampton. The various ingredients, principally sea mud and chalk, were ground and mixed in a special mixer and then put into the shallow bays that had been used years before for the collection of salt. The mixture was left for a time for the water to evaporate, and when stiff was wheeled to a large firebrick floor. This floor had several fires underneath it and when the mixture had reached a suitable state it was broken up, put in a kiln, burnt and then ground very fine. The cement was considered to be of a very good quality. At the back of the drying shed was a large square chimney about forty feet high, to take away the smoke and fumes. The foundation could not have been very good, for a short time after it was built it fell across several sheds and smashed them, fortunately without injuring anyone.

There was also an iron smelting works at the "factory" and in 1867 Mr. James Dickinson first came to Warsash as manager of these works, which belonged to Harrison Ainslie and Co. As a boy, I often went with other boys to see the iron run — a fascinating sight. This was done every twelve hours I will describe the iron works as I remember it.

The road into the factory was from the Newtown Road at the Cutting. The road is still there, but it has now been turned into a carriage drive. The foundation of the furnace is on the right side of the road. The furnace was round, and a very large one, and was built in firebrick, tapering from the bottom, till at the top it was about half the size. On the opposite side of the road was a large shed in which the fuel, iron ore, etc., were stored. Overhead was a covered way connecting the shed with the furnace, along which the materials were wheeled in barrows and tipped into the furnace. Near the furnace was a door in the wall, usually open, and it was the delight of boys to stand and watch the great flywheel with cranks moving two long arms which worked the bellows and forced the wind into the fire, thus getting the terrific heat necessary to smelt the ore. Adjoining the furnace was the moulding shed. The greater part of the floor was covered with black sand, in which the moulds were formed into which the melted iron was to run. First the men with long-handled hoes would rake the surface of the sand until it was quite smooth, then with a v-shaped piece of wood attached to a long handle, which they would draw carefully across the sand, they would make channels of the requisite width and depth, all the cross channels being connected with one main channel from the furnace. Each channel was now stamped with the letters L.O.R.N. by means of an iron stamp.

In passing we may note here the derivation of the name Lorn Villa, in which Mr. James Dickinson lived.

When everything was ready, the foreman gave the word, the big lumps of clay blocking the outlet from the furnace were removed, and the iron would run out like water, throwing off showers of sparks that flew as high as the roof. One man, with a big tool, would dexterously turn the liquid iron into all the cross channels as it ran down the main one It was allowed to cool down and later broken into lengths suitable for stacking ready for transport. These lengths were known as pig-iron. It was very hot work and even the lookers-on would be glad to get out of the shed into the cool air. Visitors came from near and far to see this sight. I was talking with Mr. J.R. Dickinson, son of Mr. James Dickinson, and enquired why iron ore should be brought all the way from the north to be smelted. I had climbed into the carts which brought the ore from Fareham, and the load always seemed to be a very small one. This was, of course, due to weight of the ore, and the carter could only do two journeys a day. Mr. Dickinson explained that at that time the wood from which the charcoal was made was very cheap and abundant in the south. Large supplies could be obtained on the Hamble river and nearby. To the cheapness and accessibility of the wood was due the presence both of the chemical works and the smelting factory. I have been informed that in the woods between Botley and Swanwick, forty men were employed as cutters and carriers. In 1882 the chemical works failed and this vitally affected the supply of charcoal for the smelting and supplies had to be brought from Wales. Shortly after, the smelting works were closed down, and Mr. James Dickinson was transferred to the works at Newland, near Ulverston, Lancashire. There he remained till 1893, when he retired and returned to Warsash to spend the remainder of his days.

It is worth recording that Mr. Dickinson was the pioneer of Total Abstinence work in the village. He was a great advocate of this movement, was a non-smoker, and in the button-hole of his coat could always be seen the small piece of blue ribbon with a white line through the middle, which was the badge of the militant non-drinker and non-smoker in those days. He was a Good Templar, a Band of Hope worker, and was also Secretary of the Congregational Church and superintendant of the Sunday School. He was a big, stern-looking man, with a long white beard in his later days, but, when you knew him, was not nearly so formidable as he appeared. A favourite way of expressing disapproval by the younger "hooligans" of those days was by a process known as "clodding". There were large grass borders to nearly all the roads and these boys would kick pieces out with their feet and pelt the object of their disapproval. Mr. Dickinson had his share, among others, but it was more dirty than dangerous, and the "clodders" were always ready to beat a hasty retreat when it appeared advisable.

Near the factory there was a creek running close up to it from the river, and a hard alongside it to the low-water point. Flat-bottomed barges could come right up to the works at high-water to load and unload, and in time the mud of the creek became so impregnated with chemicals from the drainage of the factory that no weeds would grow on it. Years after the factory was closed one or two fishermen used to lay their boats up in the creek during slack season in order to keep the bottoms clean whilst they were laying idle. The creek has now silted up, but the hard is still there and runs along by the pier that was built during the Great War for the use of the Air Service. When the land on which the factory was situated was sold, the road to it was turned into a private drive and a new footpath made to the shore. This is known as Cherry Walk. Near where this walk now ends down by the shore were some very large brick buildings, and inside these were some enormous wooden receptacles. I do not know for what purpose they were made, but they were never used. They were built on brick piers and were open to the air, under the bottom floor. Boys used to like to shout into these places under the buildings because of the queer sound it gave to their voices. Mr. E. Hills, who owned the chemical works, was a very religious man and interested himself deeply in the well-being of the little chapel and the worshippers who attended it. He built several chapels in the district where he thought they were needed.

Amongst the business men who resided in Newtown Road was Mr. Charles Sandy, the undertaker. In early times burials had to be carried out at Sarisbury or Titchfield. Mr. Phillips was the local bricklayer and lived next door to him. On the opposite side of the road lived Mr. Birch and his wife. They did the village mangling and kept a small sweet shop. The mangle was a very old-fashioned affair. The clothes were rolled around wooden rollers and a very heavily weighted box-like structure was worked backwards and forwards over the rollers by means of chains geared to a wheel with a handle for turning. When the clothes were "done" the box could be made to tip down at either end, so that the roller

at the other end could be taken out. The rude small boys of those days had a kind of doggerel verse which they used to chant to a well-known tune. The verse ran thus
"Cheer boys cheer, Mis' Birch has got a mangle,
Cheer boys cheer, it's made of wood and stone,
Cheer boys cheer, old Granfer turns the handle,
Cheer boys cheer, for they'll mangle all the clothes."

Just before we reach the end of the older part of Newtown Road a footpath leads off to the right, by the front of the old coastguard station, to the shore. One can continue on round "ship's bank" to Hook Point by bearing to the left, or by turning to the right, can follow another path to Warsash shore. Off Hook Point not far from Bald Head buoy, there is part of an ancient wreck. I am told that this vessel was caulked with moss and is a much older specimen than the one found above Bursledon Bridge.

At the far end of Newtown Road lies Hook Lake. The private footpath to Hook House was carried over it, where it narrowed, by means of a bridge. On the other side of the lake there were formerly several old cottages, and this was probably the first part of the place to be inhabited. At one time there was a good landing place there, and I have been told, and believe it to be correct, that one of the houses had a "landing right" mentioned in the deeds. Hook Lake connects with the river at Hook Point, and Hook Point appears to have been a formation made by the gravel from the cliffs at Chilling, which for hundreds of years had been washed along by the action of tide and sea. The bank thus formed from Chilling was known as High Furze, probably because of the very high clumps of furze which abounded on it. This bank extends to the point where the water from Hook Lake runs into the Hamble river. There is some evidence that the river once flowed into and around Newtown. I have seen a sketch in a book ("The Hamble River" by W.H. Trinder), which shows the lake or harbour before the bank known as "Ship's Bank" was built. The date of this survey was 1806. In later years "Governor" Hornby enclosed a large area of mudland, which stopped the water going up to the Newtown shore where there was a private quay. Part of the road from the quay to the main road is still in existence. It is believed that candles with rush wicks were made at Newtown, which gave out more smoke and smell than light. That was long before the era of safety matches, and when striking one of the old lucifer matches to light the candle it was necessary to turn the head to avoid being half choked by sulphur fumes. After candles benzoline seems to have been largely used as an illuminant (of sorts) before paraffin became general, and it was quite a common thing to hear of someone's house having nearly caught fire and the lamp having to be thrown out of doors.

The village and harbour of Hook is mentioned in Domesday

Book, and is there called "Houch" and "Hamelhoke". This harbour was used by a number of ships. A harbour further south is also mentioned. This might have been an extension of Hook Lake nearer to Fleetend, for there is reason to believe that the salt water flowed up to Fleetend. If this is so the harbour has long since disappeared. The tide has been known to overflow the banks many times. During a very high tide in 1878 the water covered the bridge near the church to a depth of more than two feet, and the bridge being merely a rough timber structure, part of it was washed away when the tide receded.

It has been handed down that Hook Point was a favourite landing point for the monks of Netley Abbey and Hamble Priory when they went to visit their brethren at Titchfield. I have been informed, and can well imagine it to be true, that in early days sailing ships caught in a gale at Spithead would run to the harbour for shelter, and that other ships coming down from Southampton and meeting the full force of the gale at Calshot, would put in here for a time until the gale abated. Some of the sailors would doubtless go ashore at Newtown and may very well have settled down there. It may be that the names of Sims Bevis Emery, Bowman and Hewett, which are among the oldest names in the district, had their lineal ancestry in some of these seamen of old. At any rate it is well known that a village existed at Hook in very early times. My information has been gleaned from various sources with so little variation in the account that one feels there must be a solid foundation of truth behind it.

At the very end of Newtown Road was the footpath leading to Hook House Hook House was built by William Hornby Esq. About 1803 the Government of that day gave him this land with the foreshore, for his work as Governor of Bombay. Mr. Hornby wished to make the property private (a trait deeply embedded in the English character) and when he built Hook House, the old village was cleared away. The house was built mainly of brick, but had a very fine stone front with stone pillars holding up a balcony. The stone appears to have been brought by sea, and was taken as near to the site of the house as possible, because some of the stones that dropped overboard still remain embedded in the mud. It was built in the true Georgian style of architecture. It was twice burnt down. After the second fire, it was left in ruins and was finally pulled down. The stables, capable of stabling several horses, are still standing. In 1869 there was a good clock on the roof of the stable and the striking of the bell could be heard for a considerable distance.

William Hornby Esq. or "Governor" Hornby, as my grandfather knew him, was born in 1773 and died in 1846. He was about thirty years of age when he first came to Hook. Arthur Hornby, his son, lived at Cold East, Sarisbury, and afterwards resided at Hook House. I remember after the new church had been opened in 1871, being taken to the lawn in front of the house and having tea with the other children of the parish. The adults were given a meat tea.

Leaving Hook House by its sweeping carriage drive, we presently came to a large iron gate fixed to square stone pillars. On either side was a aquare building, one side being used as a sleeping apartment, the other as a living room and kitchen. This lodge has now been pulled down and the gates and pillars were taken to the Fairey-Avro factory on Hamble Common and used to form the entrance to those premises. Outside where this lodge stood was a large farmhouse known as Grange Farm. This house is said to have been built in the year 1740, and the farm attached to it was of a good size. At this point there are crossroads, one leads to the shore and is called Cow Lane, one goes back to Hook House through the park, and the third goes from Cow Lane through the park, past the laundry or Pink House as it was called, and on to the Dairy. We may continue our walk along a lane which will bring us to Workhouse Land, where there are two cottages. From Workhouse Land there is a long, narrow lane through meadows to Chilling Road, and on the right, by the side of a farmyard, is a very old house, known as Chilling House, said to have been built in 1600. From here we may now pass on to Chilling copse and the fields near it, and shall see a very large pond, which was made to provide water for driving the mill. Round this mill are farm buildings and a very large house, to which several additions have been made since it was first built. This is Brownwich House.

In front of Workhouse Land is a lane by which, as its name Shore Lane indicates we may reach the shore. Over this lane there was at one time a law suit. The lane was used by men to go to the shore to collect seaweed as manure for the land, and Mr. Hornby denied the right of way and closed the lane. The case was taken to the courts and a decision given against Mr. Hornby, declaring the lane to be a right of way to the public. In 1886, in order to celebrate this victory, a large company of men, women and children, with horses waggons, carts, and a band, marched by Hook Gate, Abshot, Hook village, Fishhouse Farm, Carchels Cottage, Chilling Farm, and along the meadows to Workhouse Land cottages, finally proceeding down Shore Lane to Chilling shore, where they held a picnic. They returned home by way of the Grange Farm, through the park to Hook, and finally on to Titchfield. Apparently this so incensed Mr. Hornby that he took the case to the House of Lords and the decision was there reversed. He then closed the road.

If we now go back to Hook House and take the path across the park from the stables near the lawn, past Edney's barn to the Dairy, we are on the old track from the landing place at Hook

Point forming part of the old direct road to Titchfield, used by the monks in bygone years. At the Dairy we see the bridge over the stream, and the road leading up to the church and on to Warsash. The Dairy proper was a building behind two cottages, and children came there for milk from Warsash, Newtown, Fleetend and Hook. There was always a hurry to be first, as the early ones used to get more milk for their halfpenny. Near the Dairy was a gate across the road to keep the cattle in the park. To the right, up a short lane, are four cottages known as Park Cottages. This was also known as Pigsty Row, probably due to the fact that the pigstys were built opposite the fronts of the houses, just across the road. There was one bakehouse, and each family used to bake their bread in turn. The cottages were inhabited by the farm labourers and their families.

From the gate we can see down into the "moor" to the stream with alders lining its banks. These alders were planted all the way from Fleetend bottom to Newtown. A section of them was cut down every year by Mr. John Sandy, the woodman, and his sons, and the poles were cut in short lengths of about six feet, and the bark shaved off. In the late spring and summer some of these poles were sent to Marchwood to be used in the making of gunpowder, and some went to Southampton for the making of brushbacks, etc. When black powder ceased to be made this alder-growing industry came to an end. Travelling along the road a little further we come to another road leading off to the left. On the opposite corner is an old thatched cottage with iron-framed windows having small panes of glass. The old lady who lived there in 1869 was Mrs. Veck, for many years cook to the Hornby family. This road was the original road from Fleetend to Hook, and back in the woods a little way along it lived "Keeper" Davis and his family. A little way along this road we come to a rather steep hill known as Griggs Hill. Here it was that Mr. Peter Dimmick senior lost his life. He was taking some wood on a timber carriage down the hill and the weight was too great for the horses to hold back. It got out of control and he was run over by the timber carriage. At the bottom of the hill near the stream there was a footpath going round Helly (Hilly?) field to Hook, and another going up the hill to Fleetend. All carts and waggons from Fleetend to Hook went by way of Griggs Hill for years after the footpath round Helly field was made into a road. The Griggs Hill road has now been made into a private footpath, though the public still use it. Why it was allowed to be converted from a public road to a private footpath I have been unable to discover.

If we now go back to the top of this road and continue to the left along Hook road we come to a rather large, gabled house with wide overhanging eaves. This was called Schoolhouse, because in it was a large room that was built and used as a school for girls on the estate. The mistress was that Miss Shorten whom I have mentioned earlier. As soon as any visitor was seen coming in at the gate the girls were made to put on striped pinafores and stand in a row. As soon as the visitor entered the room, the girls would make a curtsey. Next we come to a pair of thatched cottages where Mrs. Mary Edwards, her husband and family lived. They occupied both houses for a time because of the number of her family. Her husband built himself a boat for fishing, and Mrs. Edwards used to sell the fish he caught at the big houses locally and at Titchfield.

In 1846 Mrs. Edwards went to Sarisbury to support the agitation for the repeal of the Corn Law by giving her experiences in keeping her family under it A little later on, at the invitation of Miss Eckles, she went on foot to Shedfield and spoke from a waggon, voicing the hardships suffered by millions of mothers throughout the country. She had the pleasure of hearing later that this law had been repealed. Farther along the road we come to the village green of Hook. The road turning off to the right leads to Fishhouse Farm. It was in a field at this bend that Mr. Arthur Hornby wished to build the church. On the left, at the corner, was the house and shop of Mr. George Bevis wheelwright and builder. The shop was next to the house, and had a large sawpit inside. Waggons for the farmers were built here, the ironwork being made by the blacksmith in the village. There was an open space between the shop and the next building. Here was the entrance to a meadow, and a stile and footpath leading to Fleetend. In the middle of the space was a well, from which the inmates of the cottages obtained their water. In 1863 this footpath was made into a road. There is a curious story about the origin of this road. It is said that Davis, the estate keeper, and Mr. James Gray, of Fishhouse Farm, could not agree about something on the estate, and as Mr. Gray did not like to pass Davis's house on Griggs Hill, he used his influence with Mr. Hornby to get him to make the road.

In Hook village the next four cottages were built in 1846. In front of these cottages was a narrow pavement with stone kerbing and designs worked out in black and white pebbles obtained from Chilling shore. In the centre panel of the pavement the date 1846 was worked out in these pebbles. In 1861, in the house nearest the "droke" as it was called in those days, lived Miss Elizabeth Bowman. In the next, Mrs. Mary Edwards, of Corn Law repeal fame. Then came Mr. Smith, the village cobbler who had but one leg. Then Mr. William Bowman, whose work was with the fattening beasts at Chilling. The next house was built before the cottages, and in it lived the village blacksmith, Mr. Thomas Silvester, and his sons George and William, both blacksmiths. Beyond the house was a shop with a double forge. On the opposite side of the road is a pair of modern cottages. Mr. George Silvester told me some years ago that where those cottages stand was the old thatched cottage

Bursledon Bridge

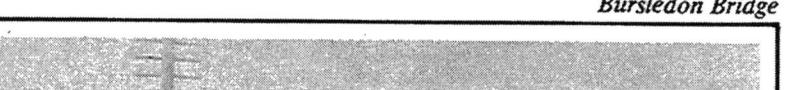

*Warsash Congregational Church and School Room
(now United Reformed)*

Tennis Party, Warsash Congregational Church

Stella Cupid, Warsash

Hook with Warsash Schools

Hook-with-Warsash School 1932/3

Hook-with-Warsash School 1907

Local housebuilding involved many specialists

Park Gate

Sarisbury Green

Fareham

and blacksmith's forge. This business has been in the Silvester family for three generations. On up the hill are two cottages belonging to Abshot House and Farm. About halfway up the road to Abshot Corner is a stile on the left and a footpath leading to Abshot Farm, Abshot House and gardens. Opposite the stile there were two very old cottages. They were pulled down in 1869. On the same side of the road, a little way on, is a meadow with a public footpath crossing it this leads to Green Lane House, and Solent Court (formerly Fishhouse Farm).

On the left we come to a bend with a good sized piece of green in the centre where the roads meet. At this point is the carriage drive from Abshot House. This was the home of the Bradshaws. The road to the left winds round some sharp bends and passes Abshot Farm, which had a very large yard. Against the road was a built-up pond, but the water got very low in the summer. In 1869 Mr. Waters was the farmer and lived in the farmhouse. Across the road is the tradesmen's entrance to Abshot House. A little further on the same side was a large pond, usually full in the winter and about half full in the summer. This pond is open to the road. The road continues on and in a short distance crosses the Warsash-Titchfield road. From the junction of the roads at Abshot the main road goes on to Hook Gate with fields on either side and a lane on the right, leading to back fields and meadows.

Going back to Hook village and taking from there the road to Fleetend, we go by the entrance to Griggs Hill, on up Hilliers Hill, and on to Green's Corner. At Green's Corner a bridle (or six feet) paths turns off to the right, leading through Fleetend bottom and joining with the Warsash-Titchfield road at the farther end. There are at Fleetend bottom two dams thrown across the stream that runs through it. These were said to have been made in order to form fishponds for the monks and nuns of Titchfield, and if this is correct they must be more than four hundred years old, and date from before the time of Henry VIII. Several archaeologists have visited these dams, and I have met them on the spot, but as far as I know, no-one has solved the mystery. Near the largest dam I have dug up three stones of the flint age. The name Fleetend has always been something of a puzzle. The natives have declared that a fleet of small boats found a good hiding place from an enemy. On the other hand, fleet means a shallow bay or ditch, and this may possibly explain the derivation of the name. A brick culvert was built at the bottom to carry the bridle path over the stream.

From Green's Corner the main road goes straight on through Fleetend to join the Warsash-Titchfield road. In Tea Tree Cottage on the right as we go along Fleetend Road, in 1874, Mrs. Ann Light started a laundry and obtained work from Holly Hill (the home of Quintin Hogg), Cold East, Warsash House, Hollham

House, Hook House and Abshot House. She employed seven, sometimes eight women. All the work was done by hand, the only mechanism being a small mangle and later a small wringer attached to a square tub. At the back of the laundry was open common, which made a fine drying ground. The laundry had a reputation through the district for doing fine work. Sometimes, when the young women were working late, the young men would gather round for a lark, but they general got the worst of it, a bucket of soapsuds skilfully distributed between them being a very effective quencher of high spirits. The policeman, who then lived at Sarisbury, would sometimes come down to see fair play, and on one occasion, whether by accident or design I do not know, he had a good bucketful all to himself. On the right of the road further along there are eight houses, formerly known as Lock's Folly, but now called Fleetend Terrace. After the Titchfield common had been shared out Mr. James Lock had the opportunity of acquiring some land near the "Jolly Farmer", and on it built these houses in three blocks. I have been told that the Jolly Farmer public-house was the first to be built after the common was enclosed in 1863.

Opposite the footpath at Green's Corner is the road through Dibles Bottom to Warsash. A little way along on the right was the lane that formerly led to Ireland Farm. It was on Ireland Farm that the first elevator was used in Warsash. It was like a straw carrier, but worked on a ball and socket arrangement. A horse was attached to a bar fixed to a cogwheel and the horse, walking round in a circle, worked the machinery. I was the first boy to be paid to drive the horse, but the horse soon learned his job, and I lost mine. This was in 1873. The wheat ricks were built on a steadle, of which there were two at Ireland Farm. They were circular in shape, supported on square dwarf piers. On top of the piers were tapering stones about two feet high, and on the top of these, flat, round-bevelled stones about four inches thick, the idea being to make the rick rat-proof. When the stones were in place, timbers about six inches thick were laid from side to centre, each joist being about eighteen inches apart, This made a good foundation to carry the weight of a very large wheat rick. When the corn was ready to build into ricks, the elevator was fixed up so that the sheave, when carried up by it, would drop in the centre of the steadle. Most farms had a man who specialised in rick-building, and took great pride in his work. I have stood all day on the rick, passing the sheaves to the builder. The waggon man would drop the sheaves on to the elevator, and as they dropped from it another man with a pitchfork would pass them on to me. My job was to stand close behind the builder and pass them to him with the butt end outward. The builder would work in two lines of sheaves, laying each sheaf so that it tied in the other. As the work got higher so the angle of the elevator was raised. Occasionally the builder went down to see that the sides of the rick were straight and true and to judge the height for topping it up. As the topping continued the apex of the rick was above the top of the elevator and a few sheaves were taken out to make standing room for a man to pass up the sheaves to the builder to complete the point. Before the advent of the elevator more men were required, two on the waggon to pitch the sheaves onto the rick, the builder, the boy, and two men to pass the sheaves and as the rick grew bigger, a building platform had to be left in the side of the rick, and the sheaves were passed from one to the other.

Four cottages were built on the side of the road and were called Ireland Cottages. From these to the farm a new road was made, and this road took the place of the old lane, which was closed in 1869.

Continuing on toward Warsash, we come to the end of the footpath at Dibles. By the side of this path are two very old thatched cottages, which originally were one From here we go on up the hill, passing the old bakery of Mr. E. Pounsett, and Furze Cottage, to the junction of the Warsash-Titchfield road, and continuing on down the road we shortly arrive at Warsash Corner again and make our survey complete, having as far as possible traversed the whole of the district.

I do not suggest that these pages containe all that there is of interest about Warsash, and it may be that I shall yet be able to make some additions to them. I did feel, however, that with so much information waiting to be collated and put together in readable form, that I should make the effort of which this history is the result.

FLEET END

The first house to be built in Fleet End was built by Mr. James Lock. Mr. John Fielder acquired it and obtained a licence to open it as a beer house. That was in the year 1863. Mr. White was the first person to occupy it, and sell beer. The house was named "The Jolly Farmer."

In front of this beer house, on the other side of the road was a pond, which was not unusual for a great many pubs were near ponds so that man and beast could quench their thirst. This particular pond went dry in the middle of summer.

Mr. George Gray who was allotted the piece of common in front of The Jolly Farmer, planted a hawthorn boundary and that enclosed the pond, and this field is today (1942) known as "Jolly Field".

In 1874, an interesting meeting was held in the skittle alley of The Jolly Farmer. I was a small boy of about eleven and I wondered what could bring so many men together and why they were so quiet. After a time, I saw two or three men coming down the road. One and another said "Yes, that's him!" and my Uncle Charlie West and Mr. Burch shook hands and had a short chat. Then the double doors of the Alley were thrown open and so they remained until the meeting was over. Then, as my Uncle was going down to the laundry to see my mother I went also, and I then knew what the meeting was about.

Uncle Charlie West was a member of the Agricultural Labourers Union. He was also a district leader. He told my mother that the special speaker was the renowned Joseph Arch. He was visiting all the villages he could. It was a very quiet meeting, very few questions were asked.

There was a journal published by the Union, and Mr. Burch, who lived in Fleet End Road was agent. He was a farm labourer and copsier. A very useful man on a farm. He was a member of the union and held to his principles, and did what he could for his fellow labourers.

When the farmers heard of this meeting they were very annoyed. Mr. Burch was discharged from the farm at which he worked, and having a family to keep could not afford to be idle. He went to other farmers in the district, but nobody would employ him although everyone knew that he was a conscientious worker and a good man to have on a farm. The farmers would give him no reason why they could not employ him, and to make matters worse, his son Alfred was discharged from his work on another farm.

Mr. Burch went quietly on. Strawberries were beginning to be grown in the district. He took up a piece of land, and eleven years after the meeting, in 1885, he built "Sea View" in Hunts Pond Road.

After a time, Mr. James Lock wanted more store room so he built up back and front with brickwork, in the open space between two blocks of houses at Fleet End. He put in a floor about seven feet high, and a stairway and roof. All kinds of ships stores were brought here and it was so used for a few years. Then changes came and the place was scarcely used.

At that time, the Hook-with-Warsash Parochial Parish reached to Hunts Pond Road, and on the West corner, at the top of Abshot Road, a new mission hall was built of brick with a tiled roof. Montague Foster of Stubbington gave the land and subscriptions were collected to build the hall.

The foundation stone was laid during a snow storm. The Choir had walked from St. Mary's, Hook, Mr. Thomas Boyes with them. This was on St. John's Day, December 27th 1886, and the building was opened for worship on St. John's Day just twelve months after.

As John was a member of the family of Mary, so the worshippers of St. Mary's, Hook, agreed that because of their effort, it would be their 'Son' and they would watch over it. The Vicar, the Reverend Henry Wilkinson Bull, appointed a Curate, the Reverend Mills Robins to take charge of St. John's. He was a very hard working man and well liked.

One day, passing Mr. Locks store in Fleet End, and seeing it almost empty, he busied himself to find out who owned it, and whether it could be rented. He got the information from a small sweet shop next door, kept by Mrs. A. Hillier.

The Reverend Gentleman was repaid for all his trouble. He got the place cleaned, and some seats and other things that were necessary, besides several good helpers.

It was made known that religious meetings would be held, inviting everyone to come.

The meetings for children as well as adults were well attended.

The Reverend Mills Robins had some happy times at Fleet End and when the time came for him to move on to pastures new, the mission at Fleet End ceased to exist, with great regret to all who were connected with this religious work.

Mrs. A. Hillier, who, I have said, had a small sweet shop next door, was beginning to want more room, and so she took over the building for a store, and a short time after, her son Winn and another lad about the same age, found it a good place to amuse themselves, especially if it was wet. Both boys had mechanical toys, such as an engine. At this particular time, they were anxious to try out a rather large engine. It was supposed to work with a small quantity of paraffin but it determined not to go. Of course there was a quantity of paper and packing stuff about. They first cleared a little larger space on the floor and put their engine in the centre. Winn knew where there was some methylated spirit a very little was put into the receptacle, a match was struck and put carefully to the spirit. The engine worked for only a few minutes, then it fell to pieces, and with the smoke and flame the two boys called for help. There was some difficulty in putting out the fire. Those two boys learned that lesson. It remained very clear in their memory.

In 1910 Mrs. Hillier got the owners of the property to put into the store a shop front suitable for larger trade. This was done, and it became a good general shop.

DIBLES BOTTOM

When I was a small boy of about eight years of age, and staying with my grandmother West in the old thatched cottage in Dibles Bottom I heard a very old man reading aloud.

I came to know it was old John Hill reading his Bible to his wife Phoebe. They lived in an old cottage near two clipped yew trees the other side of the stream. I can almost hear the old man in his slow way, saying "Verily . . verily . . I . . say . . unto. . you . ." My memory is very clear about that incident.

Mr. John Hill was a regular attendant at the Independent Chapel, he always wore a tall hat, the nap of which was always rough. In fact his dress was like a Dickens character.

There is a short lane leading off Dibles Road, known in my young day as Tooth Corner, today as Gravel Hill, leading up to what was a gravel pit and Mr. Hill's property.

The gravel from this pit with eleven other pits on the old Titchfield Common was used when the Common was enclosed, and all the roads were straightened up and repaired. It was then these pits were first used, about 1864.

Going up the lane one comes to a block of three houses built by Mr. James Gray and named Grays Cottages. They were built about 1866.

Just beyond, on the right, upon what was a big bank was Mr. John Hill's cottage.

Going about eighty yards, one came to the old bank which marked the boundary of the Old Titchfield Common. On the left, Mr. Hill built a pair of cottages, in which Mr. George Hill lived with his wife Elizabeth, known to all in the district as Gran Hill, because she was the village midwife. She lived to be ninety nine years old. She died on May 1st, 1919.

Mr. James Moody lived next door, the gardens of these houses occupied the site of the gravel pit.

On the right, at the top of the lane were set out the walls for a cottage. These were little other than clay and pieces of brick, apparently put together at odd times. They were about three feet high when I first saw them, and were crumbling to pieces.

Down the garden path were three cottages built of the same material which had been occupied for several years.

At right angles to the lane was a footpath leading to the three cottages. One stood alone, a short distance from the pair, and just beyond a meadow.

From an artistic point of view, these old cottages with the climbers on the walls, and the thatch and the box edging to the flower borders were a very pleasing sight.

Let us go inside one of these houses, they are much alike. They have been built a number of years. It was about 1873 when I first saw the inside of this house.

Mr. Tom Butler, his wife Sophie, son Jack and two daughters were living here. The front door was very narrow and low. Mr. Butler always had to bend forward to enter. Inside was a room about twelve feet square. The floor was made up of rough boards, sacks and cheap floor covering. The window was about 3 feet wide and 2 feet high. The fire was made on the hearth. The chimney and fireplace were of brickwork and very rough. The walls were faced with clay, puddled and while soft pressed together in lumps and soft clay was used to make a level surface. When this was dry, sand and lime were mixed and this was put on with a trowel. That made a hard surface. When the work was new, it was satisfactory for a cheap job.

When I saw it, wall paper, paper with pictures and brown paper had been used to cover up bad places

The ground floor was about 6'6" high to the joist, which was 4'2", on which rough boards were nailed. At one end a hole had been left about 2' square, in the centre, against the wall.

To form the bedroom, the walls back and front were about 3 ft. high and the ridge of the roof another 3 ft. making the room about 6 ft. high. The window to this room was about 2 ft. square and close under the eaves of the thatch. A curtain was strung across to form a partition. A very rough ladder was used to get to the bedroom. When not in use it was taken out of doors.

The three houses were occupied at the time of which I am writing, by Mr. Tom Butler, Mrs. Page, a widow, and Aaron "Catcher". His occupation was catching small birds such as goldfinches, bullfinches and chaffinches for cage birds. I had seen him with his net by the roadside.

About 1900 the houses I had described were cleared away and on that site a pair of well-built houses of brick with slate roofs were erected.

On the site where Mr. John Hill's cottage and garden were situated, another fine pair of houses with bay windows were built, their fronts to the lane.

PAPER BOY 1875

In recording ones own employment during the years of ones life one finds others who have gone through much the same experience.

One job I did had been done by other boys both before and after the time under review, 1875.

My real reason is to put on record what boys were expected to do for a few shillings, and at my age. I was eleven years old.

In those days there was some difficulty in getting the daily papers delivered in rural districts. The subscribers to daily papers were very few. These subscribers met and arranged to get someone to hire a boy to go to Fareham Station, get the daily papers and deliver them every day.

No doubt most of the subscribers had an interest in the Bursledon Bridge and road company.

Mr. Davis, who lived at the top of Brook Lane, Park Gate was in charge of collecting the bridge tolls, and they relied on him to get their daily papers.

I heard that Mr. Davis was in want of a boy. I told my mother of this job and had her consent to apply.

I saw Walter Merridew who had been doing the job. He said he would finish at the end of the week. I then saw Mr. Davis, who gave me the job, a list of subscribers and their addresses and mentioned that my pay would be five shillings weekly.

He said that my time at W.H. Smith and Son's bookstall at Fareham Station would be 8.00 a.m.

My home was at the Fleet End laundry and it was several years after this period when I owned a real wood and iron 'boneshaker' so it had to be done on 'Shank's pony'. I should say that I arrived home each day tired out.

It was my duty each day to call at the following addresses:
1. Heathfield House, Fareham Avenue, Sir Thomas Larcombe.
2. Catisfield House.

3. Mr. Davis, Brook Lane.
4. Mr. John Silvester, Park Gate.
5. Dr. Horn. Homeopathic practitioner at Mr. Wise', nr. Elm Tree, Swanwick.
6. Captain Turner, 'The Glen', Swanwick.
7. Captain Crawshay. To his yacht moored near Bursledon Bridge.
8. Captain Spencer Smith, Brooklands House.
9. Admiral Maxey, Holly Hill House.

On Saturday morning I called at Mr. Gough, Titchfield Post Office for a few weekly papers: The Hampshire Telegraph, Lloyds, Reynolds, Portsmouth Times.

These were to a few cottagers, and from these I received one halfpenny each, which I paid to Mr. Gough.

I was doing this job for about three months.

Recently I was shown Mr. Wynhall, the village cobbler's day book, and against Mrs. Light were six entries of boot repairs, for boy. Those were my boots in 1875.

My walk was anything but monotonous. I often had short rides. Sometimes I went Segensworth way, passing Place House, and other times, through Titchfield and "Three Stone Bottom" (this name brings to mind sayings which I have heard, I have never seen the stones, but anyone may look into the stream and select three stones and say "When they hear Titchfield Church Clock strike twelve at midnight they will turn over.")

I remember "Three Stone Bottom". I had a very sorry experience there. One fine day I was nearing the Bottom, when looking back I saw two horses and carts following me. I eased up and they soon overtook me. It was two loads of coal being taken from Fareham Station to Lower Swanwick.

The first driver asked me if I would like a ride. My bag of nicely folded newspapers was forgotten. I climbed up to the shaft, and sitting on the front of the cart it took me all my time to keep my seat, the road was so rough.

The driver reminded me I had some newspapers in my bag. Yes, I had. And, did I know how a certain horse got on yesterday?

I knew my family were averse to gambling, so I could not tell him anything, and I suddenly saw where I was.

He asked me for one of the papers. I refused because of the coal dust, but he assured me he would keep it clean. I still hesitated but I saw that he intended to have a paper, and so that I should not get them all messed up I gave him one.

With the reins between his knees he opened it wide, and his mate in the other cart questioned him about the paper. Then he told him to hold the paper with his left hand extended as far as he could. This was no sooner done than whizz! went a lump of coal through the paper. I did not ride any further. The next morning when I saw Mr. Davis he told me that one of the subscribers had not received their newspaper the day before.

HOLLY HILL

For the history of Warsash, I suppose one needs to be careful in writing about events that have occurred at Holly Hill. It is a large estate, and at one time it took in Warsash and Locks Heath as far as Locks Road, so that Warsash has some claim.

For a few years, one could get to Holly Hill by the carriage drive, over the lake in Winnards Copse but that came to an end so that now, in 1942, from Warsash by car, one must go to Sarisbury Green to get to where Holly Hill House once stood.

The estate changed hands several times in a few years and it became known as Sarisbury Court. It will not be necessary to use this name again, because what I have to say will have happened before, and in Mr. Quintin Hogg's time.

I have in my possession a Family Bible that was presented to my father, Thomas Light, by Lady Henry Cholmondely on his 21st birthday in 1847. My father worked in the garden at Holly Hill. The garden was in the valley on the south side of the house. It was a walled in garden, with a gardeners cottage, and two glass houses.

The heating system was a brick flue around the houses built on the floor. The inside of the flue was about 14 inches square and the fire was lit at one end. The flame and smoke went the whole circuit of the houses. Wood was used as fuel.

It is needless to say that the gardener in the winter had a difficult time, with storms, changes of wind and everything wet, so you will be able to see the gardeners' difficulty as it is well known that all plants either for foliage or flower had to be perfect, and changes made every morning. All this had to be done in those glass houses in the old garden with the brick flues.

There was a conservatory attached to the house, and in those times when there was wet or stormy weather, or a few minutes to wait for the carriage and pair to come round to the front door, this time was passed in the conservatory, admiring the flowers.

This conservatory is now in the centre of the new garden, between the modern glass houses.

I have seen it on record that Lady Henry Cholmondely was often seen taking her favourite walk down the lane now named Brook Avenue, and to visit Mrs. Swinton at Warsash House.

To do this, after leaving her home she would go down past the ice house near the old garden, across the meadow over a small bridge over the stream, through a wicket gate, up through Cawtes Copse (this path divided Winnards Copse from Cawtes Copse), and then through another wicket into a field called Barnes Field. There are records to show that this field belonged, in 1697, to John Warner. Of the times I am writing the field was farmed by Mr. Cawte of Brook Farm.

After leaving the gate, her Ladyship would follow the path until she arrived at Barnes Lane.

Today, 1942, there is, opposite where the stile was at the end of the path, a pair of houses. The names of these are "Glenmore" and "Tinalu".

Lord Henry Chomondely used to visit Mrs. Swinton at Warsash House. His Lordship was interested in the religious revival in connection with the Church of England.

His Lordship was a patron. He had some difficulty in explaining the revival to Mrs. Swinton.

It is recorded that Admiral Frederick Augustine Maxey acquired the Holly Hill estate from Lord Henry Cholmondely about the year 1868, and held it for about 12 years until August 1st, 1879, when it was sold to Mr. Quintin Hogg. I have related in another part of this book that the Admiral had laid out a large piece of the common for allotments.

After Mr. Hogg bought the Holly Hill Estate in 1879, about a year after the old house was burnt down, he had begun to make alterations, and a great many men were taken on. I went, and applied to Mr. Bayley the gardener for work in the garden and got a job.

The new garden was being walled in by Mr. W. Phillips, builder of Warsash. During that time, as Mr. Hogg owned the foreshore, he obtained permission to build a mud bank from the Holly Hill Hard, in a line to the end of Crableck Bank.

Before the bank was built, when the tide was out the general public walked below the natural bank. If that was not passable, they used the path along the field and through Downkiln Copse. I have walked it before the mud bank was thought of.

It was about this time that a firm of landscape gardeners began work on the stream to the East of the house, and by the side of Winnards Copse, which became eventually a great ornamental lake with rocks, waterfalls and islands planted with flowering shrubs and rock plants, and with several kinds of water bird living on its water.

There was an ornamental bridge for the carriage drive to go over from the house up through Winnards Copse to the Warsash Road, now known as Barnes Lane, which made the journey much nearer to the Big House than going to Sarisbury Green (note — there was a time, not many years before when wheeled traffic from Warsash had to go to Park Gate to get to Holly Hill House.) When Mr. Hogg sold the house and grounds, Mr. Winn bought all the South East property including the lakes, and of course this closed the carriage drive to the public. About 1890.

The new building was rearing its head above the trees and shrubs. While this was being done, a number of men were working on the lawns, removing trees, and getting a cricket field ready because it was one of Mr. Hogg's hobbies.

The gardener appointed one man, Nat Fielder, in charge of three men. I was one of them. Our job was to see all grass mown and swept, the cricket field ready, and the practise nets ready for bowling.

It was my job, with a boy named Epps, who brought a big horse from Farmer Furney, to draw a 2 ft. 6 inch grass cutter.

Mr. Hogg employed a left hand professional bowler named Roberts, a Gloucesters professional.

I feel I must record this. I, with the other three men were mowing with scythes close against the South side of the house and I was nearest the steps from the door.

Mr. Hogg came out on the steps, he asked if I could tell him the whereabouts of a certain man.

I began "I think . . . ." and irritated, "You don't know!" he said. "When you are asked a question, don't say 'I think", say 'No' or give the answer to the question." All the years since I have never forgotten that lesson. Mr. Hogg was a real gentleman. Whenever I pass his monument in London, I remember what I have just written and I take off my hat to him.

His son, Douglas, Lord Chancellor Lord Hailsham, I often saw when he was home from school, He was about fourteen years old.

In the new stables there was stored for a few years a large glass case with two tigers, stuffed. The last time I saw them they were in the museum at Netley Hospital, where they filled a very large space.

In regard to the water for the house and garden, for the previous owners wells would supply, but for the number of people that would be about the house, and more to come, there would be a great quantity of water required. Mr. Hogg had planned to have a number of young men that were connected with the London Polytechnic, week by week during the Summer.

The first arrangement was a Ram cistern in the meadow above the old garden. This worked very well, but would only supply a small house requirement. Another Ram was put over at Crableck and a powerful engine to pump the water up to the house. The water was collected from three springs.

In 1882 the mansion was completed, and then a new wing was built to give more room for all those young men who came down for a week's holiday.

On February 15th 1881 there was a tea in the new Iron Church in the corner of an orchard on the right hand side of Holly Hill Lane, going down, at Sarisbury Green.

This church was removed, whole, across the top of the Green to the position it now fills (1942). This work was done primarily by Mr. James Newbury and his sons, about 1891.

This church was a present to Sarisbury Free Church from Quintin Hogg. That is only one of the things that Mr. Hogg is remembered by.

Now I have to relate one of the saddest things that can befall such grand people as Mr. & Mrs. Hogg and their family. Their country home, that beautiful house with all its future prospects was destroyed by fire in 1886.

In a few hours the mansion was gutted. Only the walls stood.

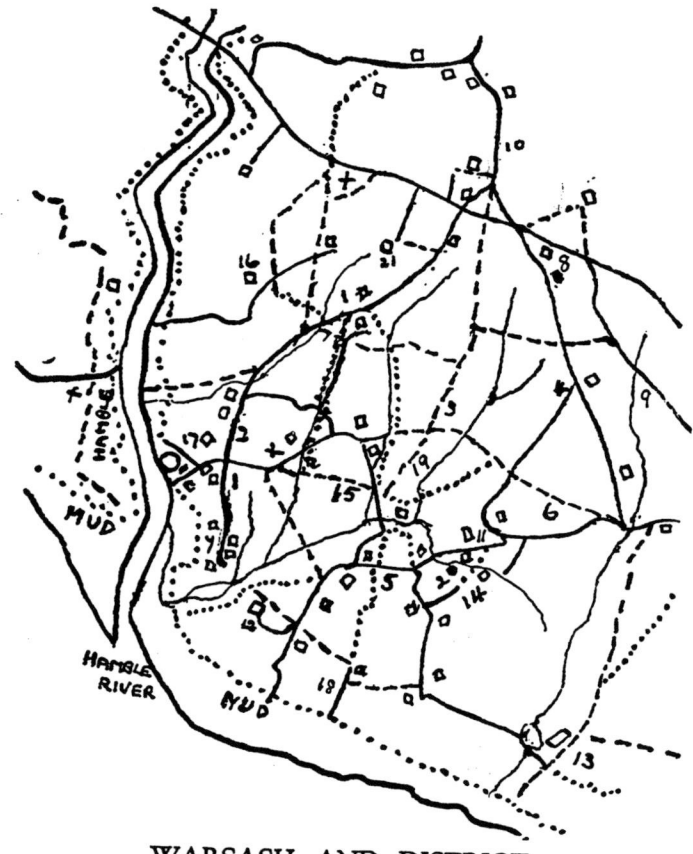

WARSASH AND DISTRICT

Roads, Cart Tracts, Footpaths and Houses existing in the Year 1864.

Tract - - - -   Roads ———   Footpaths . . . . .
    Houses ▫ ▫   Scale one inch to the mile.

1. Warsash Corner
2. Brook Lane
3. Locks Road
4. Hunts Pond Road
5. Hook Road
6. Titchfield Road
7. Newtown Road
8. Southampton Road
9. Three Stone Bottom
10. Beacon Bottom
11. Abshot
12. Hook House
13. Brownwich
14. Green Lane
15. Dibles
16. Holly Hill
17. Warsash House
18. Shore Lane
19. Fleet End
20. Village of Hook
21. Cold East House